Voices for the Land II

*Minnesotans Writing about the Places They Love
and the People Who Taught Them to Care*

Copyright © 2001 by 1000 Friends of Minnesota

ISBN 1-57131-288-9

Distributed by Milkweed Editions
1011 Washington Avenue South, Suite 300
Minneapolis, Minnesota 55415
(800) 520-6455
www.milkweed.org

Cover Art by Betsy Bowen

Dedication

We dedicate this edition of Voices for the Land to Sam Morgan and Kay Cram. Their commitment to preserving and exposing people to the wonders of natural areas is an inspiration to all of us. We will miss them. Two short tributes to these special friends of Minnesota follow:

A Passion for Parks and Trails

"What an indomitable man," I thought. I had just visited him in the hospice, where he was propped up in bed. He was still engaged in his favorite subject: He wanted to talk about Grey Cloud Island and how to have as much of it as possible declared a state park. After forty years as a parks and trails advocate, now approaching his last days on Earth, Sam Morgan's passion had not abated.

Minnesota has lost a prodigious champion of the natural world. He was a visionary and an astute tactician in one. He was a tenacious, dogged doer. Sam was also (sigh) a bit loquacious. But, we are all the wiser for bending him our ear.

The next time you gaze at the Saint Croix River from a lofty hilltop in Afton State Park,

or wander the trails of upper O'Brien State Park on a crisp autumn afternoon, or glide effortlessly along Gateway Trail on your bicycle,

or explore nature's sanctuaries at Fort Snelling State Park,

or walk the Cannon Valley Trail alongside rushing water,

or enjoy some other hallowed park ground that Sam had a hand in acquiring for the public, think of this man and what he has done for you and for generations to come. Parks and trails do not just happen. They are the products of tireless efforts by dedicated citizens like Sam Morgan.

—Peter Seed

Homage to Kay Cram

They say it's a good thing to wear well the path to a wise person's front door.

I am grateful that I went to Kay Cram's door often, and that my daughters, Katie Rose and Anna, had Kay in their lives. She was a strong example of how to be proactive and thoughtful and to live gently in life and on the land. Natural beauty didn't just move Kay: she believed it to be essential to a well-lived life.

Whether they realize it or not, there are many others like me wiser in the ways of the natural world because of Kay. As a young girl at her Hillaway Camp, I remember well that long, winding, dark, treacherous, toe-breaking, wood tick and poison ivy infested, often muddy and always mysterious path between upper and lower camp. Kay believed it was important for us white-sneakered, bare-legged campers to walk it every day.

Kay was a pioneer. She was one of the first people in the metro area to protect her land from future development by placing it in a land trust. From my time as a child at Hillaway until she died, Kay's generosity inspired me, and even though she is gone, her spirit is still with me. She is the snow on a maple tree branch. She is the sound of a hard rain beating down on my roof. She is the robin's song in the spring.

—*Lisa Ringer*

Voices for the Land II

Northwest Region

"Another Minnesota" *by Mark Vinz*	2
"The Perfect Place" *by Eric Langmaack*	4
"Heavenly Acres" *by Margaret Adelsman*	6
"Potable Lake, Hubbard County" *by Maureen Gibbon*	8
"Old Man Stand" *by Doyle Turner*	10

Northeast Region

"Spirit" *by Joanne Hart*	14
"Frog Girl" *by Laura Carr*	16
"The Horizons of Reverend Cliff" *by Forrest Johnson*	18
"Richard" *by Linda J. Hommes*	22
"Ole, Wilderness Guide" *by Tim Magee*	24

Central Region

"Can of Worms" *by Will Weaver*	28
"The Best Camping Trip Ever" *by Nicholas Bingham*	31
"The Farm" *by Kayleen Larson*	33
"The Pines" *by Sue Leaf*	35
"George Friedrich's Forgotten Park" *by Edward Weir and Eve Wallinga*	37

Metro Region

"Friends of the Natural World" *by Freya Manfred*	42
"The Median" *by Mary Bowmann*	44
"In the Heart of the Heart of the City" *by Margaret Miles*	46
"My Lost Paradise" *by Mai Nguyen Haselman*	48
"The Nature Lady" *by Barbara Lewis*	51

Southern Region

"The Teachers" *by Florence Dacey*	54
"Prairie Marsh Farm" *by Jason M. Frank*	56
"Marsh Song" *by Robert Hartkopf*	58
"The Oak Grove" *by Eve Webster*	60
"The Sight of a Lifetime" *by Rod Broding*	62

Acknowledgments

1000 Friends of Minnesota extends its deepest gratitude to the forward-thinking women who first envisioned *Voices for the Land*—Wendy Bennett, Jeanne Campbell, Gayle Peterson, Hollis Stauber, and Elly Sturgis. We also extend our sincere appreciation to the Bush Foundation and Elly Sturgis for their generous financial contributions that will help sustain the program in the future. We also thank Jan Zita Grover and Gayle Peterson for their help designing the second-round essay question and Debbie Meister for her sage advice and tireless work. *Voices for the Land II* could not have been accomplished without the patience, knowledge, and insight of our contest judges: authors Jan Zita Grover and Marybeth Lorbiecki, and *Star Tribune* commentary editor Eric Ringham.

Special thanks go to Milkweed Editions and Sid Farrar for providing technical and editorial support; to Betsy Bowen for the cover art that so beautifully conveys the value and importance of our natural places; and to Brian Peterson and the *Star Tribune* for bringing the *Voices for the Land* essays to a wider audience in the Sunday edition of the paper's Variety section. Brian's photographs have provided the perfect visual complement to these heartfelt essays about special Minnesota places.

1000 Friends of Minnesota also appreciates the unsung *Voices* work of interns Cynthia Leck and Rebecca Wienbar.

Introduction

Since the beginning of the *Voices for the Land* project in 1999, we have collected more than fifteen hundred essays from all over Minnesota. This intense and widespread interest is a <u>clarion</u> call from the people of Minnesota declaring their personal stake in our state's special places. It is a message that something more must be done to ensure that future generations have these places to visit, to share, and to write about.

The threats to the areas described in these essays are real. From 1982 to 1997, the Twin Cities experienced a 25 percent increase in population and in turn suffered a 61 percent increase in developed acres. It is estimated that approximately four hundred thousand more trucks and cars will crowd our region's roads in the next twenty years. And these threats are not limited to the Twin Cities. In 1950, Minnesota had roughly three hundred thousand farmers. Today, there are fewer than eighty-five thousand, and only fifteen thousand of them make their living from the farm alone. More and more farmers are becoming dependent upon second jobs found in the towns and industrial centers around their farms. Trends show that over the next few years, farmers by the thousands will continue to get out of the business.

Voices for the Land II continues the tradition of the first volume in providing a forum for the interplay of the arts, community involvement, and concern about the land. Some of the essays speak of mentors and everyday heroes of land preservation. Many of them contain a theme of learning about a land ethic or passing on such traditions. Some of the essays describe the anger, grief, or fear over the impending destruction of a cherished landscape. But the common thread in each essay is a genuine appreciation of natural places and a concern for how quickly they are disappearing.

New to the second phase of *Voices for the Land* is an effort to channel the passion of the essayists and like-minded neighbors into civic involvement. We will try to translate the passion and concern in these essays into work in communities throughout Minnesota, work that increases people's knowledge of and involvement in land use decisions locally, regionally, and statewide.

—1000 Friends of Minnesota

Northwest Region

Another Minnesota

Mark Vinz

From my childhood in Minneapolis to the time I moved back to Minnesota in the late 60s after living in Kansas and New Mexico for a few years, my image of rural Minnesota marched to the "sky blue waters" drumbeat of the Hamm's beer commercials. But the job that brought me back was in Moorhead, in the prairie country of the Red River Valley—so flat and uninteresting to me I found it hard to believe it was a part of Minnesota at all. Its saving grace was a fifteen mile drive east from Moorhead on U.S. 10, just past Buffalo River State Park, where the road rises up to cross the ancient beaches of Lake Agassiz and the rolling hills and lakes begin.

But then, because our wives had become friends through their work in the League of Women Voters, I came to know Brom Griffin, at that time manager of Buffalo River State Park. When Brom discovered how little I knew about the region, he invited me to join him one evening for a walk through the tract of virgin prairie just south of the park—an experience that changed forever my perspective of Minnesota.

Brom made it possible for that piece of land I'd so often driven by and ignored to come to life. His excitement in pointing out the great variety of wild-flowers and other plants was truly contagious, as were his stories of buffalo wallows and Indian camps and early settlers. It was then I must have realized for the first time that I was living in the midst of a fascinating landscape—not of the picture-postcard variety, but one in its own way every bit as profound and enduring. As we stood there at dusk among the big bluestem and coneflowers, the cinquefoil and prairie plum and old man's beard, the sky was more immense than I'd ever imagined—from an ocean of scudding clouds to one dense with stars. More than once I caught myself holding my breath in wonder.

Since that first visit, I've made many more to the Bluestem Prairie Scientific and Natural Area (as it's now called) and to other tracts of irreplaceable virgin prairie preserved in this region. Trying in my own way to become the kind of guide for others that Brom Griffin (who now works at St. Croix State Park) was for me, I've continued to learn about the prairie's fascinating biology, geology, history, and the rich tradition of literature it has inspired. And I keep coming back, delighting in its understated and ever-changing beauty, its fragile complexity so full of surprises—which I know now will reveal themselves only to those who take the time to get out of their cars and learn to see what's all around them.

Mark Vinz is a professor in the English and M.F.A. programs at Minnesota State University in Moorhead. He is the author of several books of poetry, including two collaborations with photographer Wayne Gudmundson, Minnesota Gothic *and* Affinities. *Mark lives in Moorhead with his wife, Betsy, and has two grown daughters, Katie and Sarah.*

The Perfect Place

Eric Langmaack
Age 11

The blue river flows as if it is chasing something. You see the sparkling water as you look down the hill. When you enter the river the water slowly ripples away in rings. The fish come toward you as though they were your friends.

As you ascend from the water your clothes get heavy and feel like they are weights tied to your body. You then get a chill from the cool summer breeze gently brushing against your wet clothes and skin.

As you walk through the forest you can feel and hear the sticks cracking under your feet. You also can hear the birds singing their lovely songs as if they were a choir. Though your clothes begin to dry and feel a little lighter with every passing minute, you feel tired. By the time you are completely dry, you are exhausted from hiking through the forest, and you decide to take a nap under a big oak tree.

When you wake up you leave the forest and walk home through the fields of corn. As you go through the field you can smell the strong sweetness of the corn. With every step you take you trample the corn in front of you. You are really hungry, and grab some fresh ears.

At last, you see the farmhouse and can smell the fresh blueberry pie cooling on the windowsill. As you get to the hogpen you toss some of your corn to the pigs lying in the mud. You feel obligated to save some of the corn for the horses, and they trot gracefully toward you as you hold it out.

This is my place, my grandma's farm—more than fifty acres of peace, comfort, and relaxation.

Eric Langmaack is eleven years old and enjoys bowling and playing soccer. He also enjoys playing with his friends, and when he grows up he wants to be a lawyer, writer, or professional soccer player.

Heavenly Acres

Margaret Adelsman
1st Place

As I run around a small lake near my home, winter's signature snow piles mingle with melted pools, announcing the coming spring. Despite these frozen vestiges, the call of an unseen red-winged blackbird proclaims its joy and launches reflections of my childhood home north of Bemidji. There, blackbird songs ring out from a treasured lakeside retreat, a poignant auditory symbol of a place my father lovingly refers to as "Heavenly Acres."

I wondered, as a small child, where this mystical place was that Dad called Heavenly Acres. We moved to the hundred-acre forest and water playground when I was three, and I spent some time wondering when angels would appear. Over the years, I have come to respect and treasure the land that was immediately special to my city-raised father.

Heavenly Acres was my childhood playground, providing venues for swimming, fishing, hiking, sledding, and cross-country skiing. It was my first biology teacher, sharing its bountiful but fragile ecosystem throughout the varied Minnesota seasons. It provided delicious morel mushrooms and northern pike for our dinner table. It became the auditorium for my first symphonies, sung by mystical loons, accompanied by an amphibian choir, and lighted by brilliant star-filled skies or an occasional aurora borealis. It was a source of solitude and privacy for personal introspection, lifting the worries of daily life and enlightening the soul.

From the wooden dock on the lake I would absorb the surrounding aquatic world, smelling the subtle fragrance of water lilies, hearing red-winged blackbirds converse amidst the cattails, and watching the parenting skills of loons as their new baby snuggled atop its mother's back. My sisters and I would steal forbidden moments of sun worship in this spot, and we camped in my grandparent's old umbrella tent near the water's edge.

In a world of shrinking wilderness and new definitions of "refuge," the name "Heavenly Acres" and this place of my growing-up take on renewed significance and appreciation. My children now stand on the dock of my childhood. They explore the woods, the pond, and the beaver-cut trees as I once did. Heavenly Acres continues its lessons, its concerts, the sharing of its bountiful gifts to students new and old. I return there often as an adult, and the child within runs to the lake with my boys to visit its old friend and mentor, to experience anew the outdoor embrace of Heavenly Acres.

Margaret Adelsman grew up about ten miles north of Bemidji. She has been a research molecular biologist and now, with her husband, Bruce, is raising two sons and running a home business—an internet website called skinnyski.com, which features cross-country skiing in the Upper Midwest.

Potable Lake, Hubbard County

Maureen Gibbon
2nd Place

In this land of ten thousand lakes, why do so few people swim?

Many days, I'm the only person swimming the potable waters of this lake in Hubbard County. From June until August, I swim once, twice, six times a day. Kids splash around their parents' or grandparents' dock, but most of the time I'm the only adult in the water. Truth is, lots of Minnesotans want to live by the lake, but they don't want to go in the water.

When I swim, the water is right up against my skin. It laps at my eyes even though I wear my glasses when I swim. (Haven't bought prescription goggles yet.) When I float, lake water runs into my ears and sometimes up my nose. On a bad stroke, I sometimes swallow a mouthful, sputtering. I don't worry too much about it—after all, the lake is *drinkable*. And you can bet your bottom dollar at the Bingo Palace that I want it to stay that way. I care about clean water because it's in my face.

Here's my theory. If I love this lake without swimming in it, something dangerous can happen. If the lake is *there* and I'm *here*—on the dock, or in a boat, or whizzing around on a jet ski—I'm removed from the very thing I love. It's that remove, that distance, that can fool me into thinking that a *little* pollution is OK.

But a little pollution isn't OK. Even a little bit of fertilizer to keep a lawn green is deadly to the lake; it causes algae growth. Removing ice ridges, tearing out native vegetation (which is both a filter system and an anchor against shoreline erosion), and filling in wetlands in order to get more buildable land all negatively impact water quality. If I do any of these things, I'll have to face, head on and eyes stinging, the very real consequences of my actions. So will loons, turtles, and fish. Swimming forces me to make decisions that will keep the water clean, and it reminds me of just how clean water can be and should be.

So, get out of your boats and off your jet skis. (Take it from me, gasoline tastes terrible.) Instead, float for an hour. Dive like a loon and twirl like an otter. Let the water wash over you. Swim.

Maureen Gibbon grew up in Pennsylvania and now lives near Osage, Minnesota. Her work has appeared internationally and has been translated into French, German, Spanish, and Norwegian. She is the author of the novel Swimming Sweet Arrow, *published in the U.S. by Little, Brown.*

Old Man Stand

Doyle Turner
3rd Place

There are stories that run by a giant white pine just south of memory. Their trails are as worn as deer trails. Deer have run by that tree for years. That tree is a trail marker for deer. It is a story marker.

Look to the west and the light from the setting sun weaves through the popple stand reaching toward you from the lake. The ground is always littered with leaves layered crisp, then damp as coffee grounds running down the side of your boot as you clear off a spot. You stand as quiet as that massive tree, silent but for the whispering of an upper-atmosphere gust. You stand beneath a tree that has been there for your relatives, there even before the ones you can remember. Your eyes scan the change from popple stands to hardwood-covered hills. Your eyes know to "look as far as you can" into the woods as the old man has told you, as his old man told him. You can hear the echo from your great-great-grandfather's voice. As you look for movement, your thoughts slow. You tell yourself stories to keep out the wind, the cold, the stillness humming in your muscles.

Underneath that tree, at the crossroads of trails, you retrace the plots of the old stories about people you don't know, people whom you've met only in story. You see them stuck in their same predicaments, struggling their same struggles over and over again, as long as you are willing to keep telling the story. You see where your uncle faced the wrong way, the animals going behind him. In the middle of one of the best and oldest stories, you think you might have heard a sound. Was it real, or is this an echo from the story? You're a pretty good storyteller yourself. You're back to yourself complete with stiff muscles that beg to stretch out on a walk, just down the hill. Then you remember, *never leave your stand.* How many stories have taught you that? Wait for the whistle from the driver, the one to call you out. *Never leave your stand.* You sink back into your thoughts, your mind tallying the stories as they pass, poking their ribs to see if they're ready to tell again. You'll never leave this place, this Old-Man's-Stand-becoming-your-stand. You carry it with you as a trail marker for stories, a signpost to your past.

Doyle Turner comes from Naytahwaush on the White Earth Indian Reservation in northwest Minnesota. He is an enrolled member of the White Earth Nation, Mississippi Band. Doyle teaches writing and literature to seventh grade students in Bemidji, where he resides with his wife, Molly, and their two children, Tony and Sophia.

Northeast Region

Spirit

Joanne Hart

When I began living on the Grand Portage Reservation in the pines by the Pigeon River, I realized I needed to learn about the Ojibwa people here and about how they saw the natural world around us. I could identify many birds and plants and knew a bit of Native American history, but when the elders, always with patient courtesy, allowed me to ask questions, even ridiculous ones to their ears, they showed me another view of the world.

I spent many hours asking Herman about fishing in Lake Superior, Waus-wa-goning Bay. His Scandinavian father taught him the skills of boats on the lake, nets, seasons of fish. His Ojibwa mother gave him insight into the spirit of what he saw and did. To me, eagles were beautiful, huge, endangered birds, but to Herman they were intimately connected to his life. When bad weather kept him from pulling the day's nets, the spoiled fish had to be dumped, and eagles dropped from rock cliffs by the bay to feast. Seeing this, Herman began regularly tossing part of each day's catch into the water for the eagles. One day, Old Walter asked him, "Did you offer yet?" Herman hadn't thought of it, but that night he dreamed how to make a tobacco offering on the lake at dawn. Then late in the evening after his first offering of *ah-say-ma,* he heard a sound just as he was falling asleep. Thinking someone had come in, he checked, found no one, but in his sitting room hung layers of tobacco smoke, a sign the eagles had accepted his gift.

And there was Wilfred, who told me owls are scary, which was not the idea of owls I'd absorbed from A. A. Milne. When he was a child, every April his grandmother's sugarbush became a family camp to harvest rising maple sap. One night Wilfred and the others heard an owl call. The sugar camp got very quiet. Next morning the children found an owl, long dead, just feathers, bones. No one talked of it, he said, nor speculated who was the dead one who cried in the night.

I think often of what Raymond said when I mentioned that the river was my water supply: *If you drink the Pigeon, you'll never grow old.* He wasn't just teasing me, of course, he was right. Here I am, twenty-five years later, discovering, again and again, the spirit that underlies everything I used to call reality.

Joanne Hart, a poet who lives in Minnesota's Arrowhead, is the author of three chapbooks and Witch Tree, *a collaboration with visual artist Hazel Belvo.*

Frog Girl

Laura Carr
Age 18

My clean, washed, city feet slide into the cool water. Lake muck oozes between my toes. I hunch down into a ready position. I am transformed into yet another animal, equal to all other inhabitants of this earth. No longer am I the city girl wrapped up in my studying, my friends, and myself. I am like the heron, ready to strike. I see the familiar glisten off the back of my prey. The sun warms my neck. Lifting my feet carefully in and out of the water, toes in first so as to not make a ripple, I advance slowly, silently, slipping my hands into a cup around the slimy amphibian. Holding it in my grip, its legs in my palm, the small frog looks at me and blinks his clear eyelids. Later, as I watch it leap back into the water, I think, *How lucky you were to be seized by me and not the hungry heron!* My little sister stands by, enthralled by the ease of my capture. She will learn soon.

    I had spent the summers of my childhood immersed in the swampy waters of the shores. Years since my last capture, I can still remember perfectly my practiced procedure of "frogging," as my family called it. I was the frog girl. Now this frog girl is nearly done with high school, driving, working, and seemingly immersed in her own life rather than the waters of old. Yet, I will always have the memories of the summers spent at my cabin.

Truly understanding this life can be achieved only when one understands its fragile balance, a balance in which we play a vital role. I was lucky and experienced this balance at my cabin. For the rest of my life I will remember and understand the balance of life and respect it, just as I will always remember how to catch the frog.

My family is trying to keep our land for future generations to enjoy. It is crucially important for the preservation of our environment to save all the disappearing natural areas we can. It is unthinkable that we should let our beautiful landscapes slip away like minnows through our fingers. We must join together and stop the destruction of our Minnesota forests, plains, waters, and wetlands. Only then will future frog girls be given the same opportunity to gain a real understanding of wildlife and a genuine awe for nature.

Laura Carr is a senior at Duluth East High School. Laura's family includes her parents, Jim and Mary, and her younger sisters, Karen and Hannah. Her interests are singing, athletics, writing, and the outdoors.

The Horizons of Reverend Cliff

Forrest Johnson
1st Place

A significant line of houses had crept within the sight of Reverend Cliff's small wooden shack that sat in a field long roped off by surveyor's ribbons. Though he was ordained only by the local kids and the few farmers long since gone, and professed no faith other than to "the Big One that looks over all life," as he put it, Reverend Cliff had always known it would only be a matter of time before nearby residents began to complain of the visual eyesore the crooked shack and its crooked steeple with a single window presented to them and their new lawns and cars and decks that overlooked his creek. He had always understood that, soon enough, the town council and the mayor with the shiny hair and a developer or two would come by and sit him down and explain the expediency of him and his nonexistent congregation selling out and moving away.

 Cliff would often sit above the edge of Lake Superior on the tablelands that had been sculpted by lava flows and glaciers and the cutting of the pine, and shake his head. He would say he never thought that such change would invade his small corner of the world where the ravens and grosbeaks had always been his only true neighbors. He loved the birds and at eighty-three years old, he himself was shaped like a blue heron, if you can picture a heron that pretty much lived on molasses and peanut butter sandwiches.

"When I die I'd like to be a perching bird or a woodpecker," he once said, knowing what he looked like as well as anyone. "But if I end up poking along in my creek with my toes down in the mud that'll be fine. There's a certain grace and patience to a shorebird."

As the houses grew closer and the roads continued to sever a countryside sprinkled with white spruce and birches, Cliff said he tried to think of his field and woods as they were before they had been hemmed in and made into a skeleton of ribbons. But try as he might, whenever he wandered off his land and found himself in the middle of what he knew would soon be yet another busy street lined with houses, he would look back toward his shack and realize that such thoughts were becoming only memories. And no matter how hard he squinted his eyes into the distance, no matter how many times he had crossed that field using only the line of trees along the horizon as his compass, he knew that soon he wouldn't be able to bring back even in his mind what had been there before. Old black-and-white photographs that he kept in a drawer were useless. They were mere shadows, he said.

Upstream from Cliff's land a small black spruce swamp had been logged and the creek bridged with fallen timber. A gravel pit had given up its marrow and sat abandoned, bleeding red clay into the creek with the slightest rain. On nearby farmlands, gates once used to hold cattle in were now used to keep people out. Off to the east a beaver pond had dried because the rivulets that fed it had begun to be diverted into storm drains and holding ponds that were hidden like sterile children in the hills beyond the advance of the tract homes and cul-de-sacs. On walks he would point out that even cattails refused to grow along those muddy banks.

A lifelong dowser, Cliff said his bones just couldn't find water anymore. "It's a two-way street. In order to find water you've got to believe the water," he'd say. "And right now the water doesn't believe in us, I guess. I kept getting weaker and weaker signals. I even thought my willow branches were going bad but I'd never heard of that happening before. The water is just keeping its mouth shut. What little is left around here doesn't want to be found."

Still, on quiet spring nights you could hear Reverend Cliff playing his accordion above the humming of the frogs and the buzzing of the few woodcock hoping to lure a mate. Even as these once remote lands were being swallowed by the toxic myth of manifest destiny, a new sun warmed the shoots of grass strong enough to push through pavement. Cliff would climb up the six or so stairs into that small steeple and sit in a folding chair, his slight, bent body hidden by the immense accordion. The lilting of the few chords he knew would repeat over and over again, a mantralike rhapsody that made your feet shuffle and seemed to push back the years and renew the land before your eyes. The new houses were gone. The creek would flow clean and the mayor with the shiny hair and his friends the developers were boys again who fished for brook trout and built tree forts and rode their bikes through woods that they would never want to lose.

Forrest Johnson is the editor of the Lake County News-Chronicle *in Two Harbors. He writes fiction and dreams of the day when he'll give his house to his kids and move permanently to his shack located miles from the nearest road on a small creek that flows into a bigger river that flows into the biggest lake in the world.*

Richard

Linda J. Hommes
2nd Place

When I moved to Aitkin County ten years ago for semiretirement, I knew my life would change: from city to country, from busy interstate highways to quiet country roads. I also went from close-quarter neighbors to my nearest neighbor, Richard, living a mile up the road.

Tall and broad-shouldered, Richard, at sixty-seven, still lives in the same farm house where he was born. He tends a small herd of Hereford cattle and gardens from spring planting till fall harvesting. From our first meeting when I discovered our mutual interest in gardening, I knew I'd found a kindred spirit. I came to him often with questions on what and when to plant, how to harvest, can, and pickle.

In spring he asked, "How would you like to make maple syrup?" Then we began the adventure of tapping maples, gathering clear, slightly sweet sap from coffee cans, simmering it over a wood fire, and finally tasting warm amber syrup on pancakes.

In July, August, and early September he took me to his favorite haunts to pick wild blueberries, blackberries, and cranberries. I, a city girl with a country heart, was discovering the wonder of nature's bounty within a nearby bog—the thorny thickets and spongy moss of a marshy lake.

Late that August, Richard added wild ricing to my growing list of adventures. A longtime ricer himself, he taught me the traditional Ojibwa method. As Richard "knocked," I poled until green rice filled our small canoe. The golden days we spent sharing this venture strengthened our bond.

As mentor and sage, Richard has taught me more than just how-to's and locations. He's shared his abundant wealth of nature lore so now I, too, can identify the distinctive call of a sandhill crane. I know from the shrill chirping of a tree toad that rain is surely coming. I know that great sense of joy in seeing a field covered in dew-laden spider webs.

He shared his deep love of the land not just in words, but in his reverential care to preserve the spots we visited, making sure that all we left were footprints. Richard made possible many new experiences that have deepened my appreciation for all of nature and enriched my life. I'm so fortunate to have him as neighbor and friend.

A longtime Twin Cities resident, Linda Hommes, along with her husband, David, moved in 1991 to a thirty-acre tree farm in Aitkin County for early retirement. She has immersed herself in a wide range of outdoor activities, from beekeeping, peeling logs, and wild ricing to running country roads, snowshoeing, and cross-country skiing. Possessing a passion for books and a love of words, Linda enjoys writing nature essays and memoirs and has been published in the Lake County Journal *and* Aitkin Independent Age.

Ole, Wilderness Guide

Tim Magee
3rd Place

July 4, 1999. Severe Storm Causes Major Blowdown in BWCAW.

My heart sank as I read the headline. The intensity of my reaction surprised me. I had no idea the Boundary Waters had become imbedded so deeply into the marrow of my soul.

I'll never forget my first adventure through this pristine wilderness. This is when I learned about personal responsibility with seven fourteen- to fifteen-year-old boys, two YMCA adult volunteers, and a young man with a bushy, orange beard. We left Camp Menogyn on West Bearskin Lake for a week in the Boundary Waters in August of 1951. Ole, with the beard, was our guide, a big man—at least six-feet five-inches, muscular and compact.

One evening Ole told me to find some firewood. I took our ax and paddled to a stand of dead cedars. On the way back I somehow (and I still have no idea how) managed to drop the ax out of the canoe. I paddled on to the campsite and told Ole what had happened.

He looked at me for a moment and then said, "I'm going to have to dock you for the ax if you can't find it and bring it back."

I said nothing but thought, *I'm just a kid. I have no money for the ax.* I was sure I would never find the ax, let alone be able to reach it by diving. But I found it, looking up defiantly from the lake bottom in fifteen feet of water. It was on my fifth dive that I was able to grab it. I was gasping for air as I reached for the canoe. The ax nearly slipped out of my hand as I struggled to get it and myself back into the canoe.

I can't begin to describe the triumph and pride I felt as I handed the ax to Ole. He hardly looked at me as he turned and continued preparing our supper.

Ole taught me that savoring the beauty and majesty of the northwoods requires courage and determination, qualities he helped me to find within myself. We must do everything we can to protect the BWCA as it recovers from the Independence Day storm. There will be fourteen-year-olds for generations ahead that will need to come of age in the arms of her wild beauty.

Tim Magee is a retired psychiatrist living on a lake in northeastern Minnesota—the area he loved as a teenager. Tim enjoys writing about the Boundary Waters Canoe Area.

Central Region

Can of Worms

Will Weaver

The idea for a fishing tournament just came to him, he said. Brainerd has one, why not Bemidji? A professional-amateur walleye "classic." Something to draw tourists, boost the economy.

He was a local man, had grown up in Bemidji. He was civic-minded, a Rotarian. He and his family lived on Lake Bemidji in a rambler home with a television dish and a wide, immaculate, fertilized lawn that ran right down to the water's edge. At dockside were the kids' two jet skis plus his own twenty-foot Pro-V Bassmaster with twin one hundred horsepower Evinrudes. It had dual electric trolling motors, Lowrance fish loctor/depth finder, GPS, live wells—Babe Winkelman and Gary Roach had nothing on his boat. He loved those cable channel fishing shows. Which was actually where he got the idea for a fishing tournament.

Organizing the First Annual Bemidji Walleye Classic was a learning experience. He was surprised to discover he needed a permit from the local DNR fisheries office. But staff there made it easy. His pitch to the Chamber of Commerce was easier still.

"I've always thought we should make more use of the lake," said the Chamber president.

"The lake should be the centerpiece of our economy," said the mayor.

An accountant projected a weekend infusion of a quarter-million dollars.

"A win-win situation," everyone agreed.

The off-season preparations were endless but energizing. All the downtown business people loved his idea. Large suppliers of high-tech fishing gear such as Cabela's and Abu Garcia got on board. Local beer companies bid for tap rights at the "Shore Lunch" tent. Everybody, including local charities, would make money.

Finally the day arrived. One hundred high-speed walleye boats idled at the shoreline, waiting for the starting gun. When the boats roared off, the crowd cheered, and the shallow water boiled with silt.

He himself was too busy to fish. There were endless interviews with the regional newspapers and radio stations. Behind him, the lake had never been busier with buzzing personal watercraft and waterskiing demonstrations. At the day's end weigh-in, fishermen hoisted their catch. There were photos. Smiles. Afterward the walleyes were released, of course. Most darted off to deeper water, though many swam slowly, and at odd angles.

On shore, he stood with representatives from Cabela's, *In Fisherman* magazine, and Waverunner Personal Watercraft. Behind him the lake was quiet now. Water glinted with small bright rainbows of gasoline. One undersized walleye, belly-up, finned weakly in silty water close to shore. "Next year's tournament will be even bigger and better," promised the man.

And everyone cheered.

Will Weaver grew up on a dairy farm in northern Minnesota. He graduated from the University of Minnesota with a B.A. in

English and with an M.A. in Creative Writing from Stanford University. He teaches and writes at Bemidji State University. As an outdoorsman, he is deeply concerned by the impact of high-tech sports gear on our natural resources.

The Best Camping Trip Ever

Nicholas Bingham
Age 15

I wake to the chatter of birds and of my fellow scouts. I hurriedly put on a change of clothes and upon exiting my tent, find our cook tent in a shambles from several waves of raiding raccoons. They've left a trail of clawed paper towels and an entire picnic table smeared with jam. At least the mosquitoes are manageable here, thank goodness; I can count the number of bites on my body on one hand.

I grab my pole and vest and head off with my friend and his father. He and I paddle while his father watches. Our laborious efforts get our aluminum craft across the lake in roughly twenty minutes. We beach our canoe in some reeds and walk onto a sandbar. Poles, mealworm, and nightcrawlers in hand, we walk out fifteen feet and cast our lines, where we catch mostly sunfish. Soon we're tired from the heat and dive from the sandbar to cool off. Then we fillet our fish, eat, swim, explore, eat, swim, swamp two canoes, raise two canoes, eat s'mores around a campfire, sleep, and do the same thing all over again the next day.

In short, this was one of the best camping rips I have ever been on. Being a kid is great, but having awesome outdoor experiences like this makes it twice as fun. If anything were to happen to the state park where we camped, be it from lack of funds, forest fire, arson, or stupid people in high places, I don't know if I would get totally infuriated or just cry.

My parents tell me not to litter, so I don't. My former teacher, Mr. Gannon, taught me to love our land and to treat it with respect. (I used to frown upon seeing *any* trees cut down, until I learned from him that clearing away larger dead trees lets undergrowth and younger saplings receive their share of sunlight and nutrients from the soil.) But it's the opportunity to go camping at places like Andy Battle Lake and Camp Cuyuna that has been the greatest blessing for me.

I want other people to have the chance to do the same. I want them to know that, even though it is hard work, it's more than no TV, no hot water, and no AC. To me, camping is the best way there is to escape everyday stress in our fashion-rocked, image-blasted, consumer-driven society.

Nicholas Bingham, a fifteen-year-old freshmen at Little Falls Community High School, wrote this essay as an assignment for his English class. Nicholas cites being part of the Boy Scouts of America as giving him an appreciation for the great outdoors and many opportunities to experience the rustic living of camping.

The Farm

Kayleen Larson
1st Place

Farms are like marriages: they require work, nurturing, and commitment. And they both tend to be overly romanticized.

My stepfather was a farmer. He loved his farm like he loved my mother. I understood neither. I was an eleven-year-old aspiring gymnast at a Twin Cities junior high and when my mother announced she was marrying my stepfather and moving us to central Minnesota to live on a farm near a town with no McDonald's, let alone a gymnastic team, I was devastated.

On the farm I tried hard not to let the smell of fresh-cut hay intoxicate me, or the softness of a newborn calf convince me that this life was better than the one in the city I had left behind. But nature has a way of drawing us in and soothing our spirits and it wasn't long before I, too, became a part of the farm's daily rhythm, rising early to feed calves, and helping unload the last bale of hay as the sun set at the end of a long, hot summer day.

By the time I left for college, my life in the city was a faint memory. I could no longer imagine what it was like to gaze on rows of houses instead of rows of corn. I wondered if I would be able to see the stars through the city lights or hear a thunderstorm over the noise. I realized that living on the farm had changed me.

Late one fall I returned. My stepfather was dying and, knowing it wouldn't be long, he had pleaded to go home from the hospital. He wanted to die on the farm. Soon after his release he and I sat on the porch watching the leaves blow in the October wind. "Like them," he said pointing to the swirling leaves, "I don't have a choice about the direction I'm going."

We buried my stepfather in a small cemetery about a mile and a half from the farm. Nice, I thought. He would still be close enough to hear the tractors moving along his acreage, to feel the warm sun embrace his Fourth of July corn, and to watch as soil from his back forty blew across his grave on a windy April morning.

The more I think about it, farms are really like life. There are good years and bad years. And the good years make it all worthwhile. I loved that farm like I loved my stepfather. And now that I'm almost forty, I think I finally understand them both.

Kayleen Larson lives with her husband, Reed, and their children on twenty-eight acres near Brainerd. She believes spending part of her childhood living on a farm is largely what motivated her to leave the Twin Cities three years ago and return to a more rural lifestyle. She is a part-time writer for a scientific association and full-time mother to her five-year-old twin boys, Erik and Sam, and two-year-old daughter, Abby.

The Pines

Sue Leaf
2nd Place

Late at night when I cannot sleep, I think of the pines. I lie in my bed, wrapping the covers close, and bring to mind their soaring silhouettes, their trunks straight and true, their graceful branches arcing upward.

The pines grow on the northern shore of Lake Alexander in Morrison County, on land my family has owned for decades. They are remnants of the vast white pine forest that once adorned a third of Minnesota's land surface. When I was a child, we gave them names: the Sentinels on the shoreline protected us; the Friend, whose needles we stroked like fur, grew close to the cabin. We thought of them as conscious then, and I still do. On sleepless nights they remain, for me, true friends and protectors.

Most of the white pines in Morrison County fell to the ax and the crosscut saw. Logging was heavy around Lake Alexander in the 1880s. In fact, an old plat map recorded a sawmill operating on our property. No trace of the sawmill remains today; we know only the sawyer's name: S. Keezer. I do not know why our pines escaped the fate of their cohorts. Surely trees within spitting distance of a sawmill would render the highest profit. I can only assume Mr. Keezer thrilled, as I do, to their stately form. On summer days when their piney scent spiced the air and the wind soughed through their silky needles, I imagined

Mr. Keezer resting in their shade and feeling their majesty. Perhaps their beauty spared them.

I have spent years steeped in the writings, teachings, and activism of heroes striving to shore up a declining environment, frantic to capture the attention of indifferent people. Yet no single act has had a more lasting impact on me than the unknown Mr. Keezer's preservation of the pines. His restraint echoes through time.

Late at night when I cannot sleep, I think of the pines. I see the way their limbs sashay in a breeze off the lake and the movement consoles me: perhaps if elegance like this can exist, there is a God who will save this planet.

Sue Leaf lives in Center City, Minnesota. She is currently at work on a collection of essays about life on the Anoka Sandplain of east-central Minnesota.

George Friedrich's Forgotten Park

Edward Weir and Eve Wallinga
3rd Place

I never met him nor heard of him until I asked the graybeards at the university about the forest east of campus: fifty acres of oak and pine woods peppered with abandoned granite quarries. Just a mile from downtown St. Cloud, it's not so much a lovely park as it is an untended piece of land, rare in this sprawling city.

A tacky pipe gate and "no trespassing" sign confront me at the entrance, which is only a deteriorating tar road. But curiosity trumps good judgement, and past the gate I walk. Seventy-year-old white pines line the north side of the road and a crumbling rock wall, right from the stanzas of a Frost poem, parallels the south. Almost hidden in the brush sits a granite boulder as tall as I am. The unadorned inscription reads: "George Friedrich Park."

George Friedrich, I learn from worn annuals and back issues of the college newspaper, was a popular biology professor from 1921 until 1950. "One of the most popular and gifted teachers in the history of the school," according to one local historian. Pictures show the quintessential professor, a handsome silver-haired teacher, conservationist, author, and proponent of what Teddy Roosevelt referred to as "the strenuous life." In 1934, Professor Friedrich persuaded the president of what was then the Teachers College to purchase the abandoned quarry land near campus.

An early disciple of the conservation movement, Professor Friedrich believed in the value of the outdoor classroom. With his students, he planted pine seedlings, stacked rocks into walls, and attended the reawakening of exploited land. He told students: "Get close to nature and you get close to God." In 1951, the college named the site in his honor.

Eventually, though, college leaders forgot about Professor Friedrich and his desire to give the college students a classroom without walls and the community a place "for a tramp through the woods." His park became the university's liability, easier to close than manage. And this is how I find it today, his handiwork still evident but neglected.

The story of George Friedrich unfolds only to those who work to find it. Forgotten and ignored, his park awaits rediscovery. What would Professor Friedrich say if he were still living? I'd like to think he would remind the university's number crunchers of the value of a place where lessons are learned in three dimensions and knowledge takes root in all five senses.

Edward Weir lives in St. Cloud, where he is tolerated by his saintly wife and two angelic children. He spends much of his time living a gentleman's retirement and contemplating his reason for being. His only other publication was a paper he was forced to write to escape graduate school, published in an obscure scientific journal he no longer remembers the name of.

Eve Wallinga was born in Racine, Wisconsin, and has lived in St. Cloud for the last fifteen years. She helped found the Sierra Club-Big River Group and the Central Minnesota Chapter of the

Minnesota Land Trust. As an environmental activist, she has worked on open space acquisition, endangered habitat preservation, and the development of St. Cloud's Environmentally Sensitive Areas Ordinance.

Metro Region

Friends of the Natural World

Freya Manfred

After he finished his writing for the day, my father, the novelist Frederick Manfred, worked outdoors on nine acres of Minnesota River Valley bluffs he and my mother, Maryanna, purchased in the early 1940s. Like the farm boy he had always been, Dad planted a huge garden of strawberries, asparagus, lettuce, tomatoes, green peppers, corn, squash, beans, watermelon, and cantaloupe, as well as iris, peonies, tiger lilies, hollyhocks, and climbing red roses. My mother also spent hours in the garden, weeding with me or harvesting the produce. She canned tomatoes, pickles, corn, and beans, and put up apple sauce, plum jam, and chokecherry jelly. I often came upon my mother down in the grape arbor, her eyes musing on the winding river in the distance, and she would say how perfect the valley was.

Beyond the garden Dad planted an orchard of apple, plum, and pear trees alongside the giant oaks, elms, and maples that already shaded our acres. I followed him everywhere, playfully lending a hand as a five year old, genuinely helping at ten, taking on even more labor as I approached fifteen. Together we set up houses for purple martins and tried to stop sparrows from taking them over. "They never should have brought those pesky sparrows over from England," Dad cried. "They chase out the native birds." When I found the hummocky wetlands below the house difficult to cross, Dad explained how vitally important bogs were to the ecological system, and how "some of our true ancestors live there: I mean the turtle, the frog, the snake, the snail, the possum and ground hog, and maybe, if we're lucky, the fox or wildcat." He pointed out that the slow, muddy Minnesota River was but a small remnant of the ancient five-mile-wide River Warren. "The bluffs where we stand were once the shores of that great river. And some of these prairie grasses on our property have been there since before the white man."

When a tall, smoke-belching factory was built across the river in Savage, my six-foot nine-inch father became taller and smoke-belching himself. He strode up and down shouting about "greedy fat cats" who "want to ruin something irreplaceable" just to "add a few more coins to their coffer." He called newspapers, spoke in protest at town meetings, and helped organize a group to preserve the valley. But in 1959, after fighting for years, he moved our family to the farmlands of Luverne, Minnesota, "where at least they won't put a factory in my backyard because they're too busy polluting the river with farm run-off. I can deal with that, and I will, too!"

I believe my father and mother awakened a love of nature in me that has as its source some deep, altruistic, empathetic well that allows all of us to participate in, and yet continually honor and protect, that which is wild, true, strong, fragile, and holy.

Freya Manfred is the author of four books of poetry and a literary memoir about her father, Frederick Manfred: A Daughter Remembers. *She's married to screenwriter Tom Pope and has twin sons.*

The Median

Mary Bowmann
Age 16

Curving in between the West River Road and Edmund Boulevard is a strip of land. Green in the summer, white in the winter, and brown every other season, this strip of land is commonly referred to as "the median." The two roads that run along the river—a major thoroughfare and a residential street—are divided by this swatch of land. *The Middle Ground.*

Yet to push this strip of green aside as merely a separation between two roads would be a mistake. Long and wide, the median is home to plants and trees, rocks and rock walls. In addition to the oaks, evergreens, and other robust bushes that dot the median, there is a hillside of protected prairie grass. In the spring these grasses and wildflowers drink up the rain and soak in the sun. The median comes to life. *The Uncommon Ground.*

This uncommon median attracts one quite common animal: the dog. Families come with babies in backpack carriers and children in tow; the one free hand guides the family black lab or golden retriever. Frail-looking elderly women with curly white hair come with tiny, curly white-haired dogs. Lean men in the prime of life run by with sleek greyhounds right at their heels. Young teenagers with responsibility on a leash walk by with young springer spaniels. Yet to all these four-legged companions, the median serves one purpose. *The Squatting Ground.*

In all seasons, the median beckons to athletes. During winter, recreational skiers on wooden touring skis groom a trail for themselves and those who come after them. The layers of deep snow keep these skiers from moving faster than a slow trudge. But before long, trudging will give way to jogging. The snowmelt forces joggers to hop and zigzag around countless muddy puddles. Soon, the puddles are gone. Jogging gives way to running. Each step wears away at the thin brown trail through the median. *The Training Ground.*

As I thrust one ski beside the other, trudging through the heavy white snow, as I place one foot in front of the other, skimming over the thin brown trail, I am assured. I know where I am. *The Home Ground.*

Mary Bowmann is a senior at Minnehaha Academy. In addition to living and going to school along the median, Mary bikes, drives, runs, walks the dog, and roller-skis along it (West River Road). Mary also enjoys volunteering in the nearby community.

In the Heart of the Heart of the City

Margaret Miles
1st Place

I live in the heart of the heart of the city. The little twenty by thirty-foot plot of grass I own with my sweetheart supports a full flock of street-tough birds—sparrows, starlings, pigeons—a dozen squirrels, one rabbit, and the occasional species that migrate through like our neighbors in the nearby apartment buildings, staying just long enough for us to get to know them by sight and then they're gone. We faithfully tend a birdbath and four feeders, even though I like to bellow daily in my best Ralph Kramden, "House and home, Alice! They're eating us out of house and home!" And then we refill the feeders.

I understand when people leave the city to "get back to nature." It is true that the freeway a block away drowns out all caws, chirps, and warbles, and the blue TV glow in a dozen windows down the alley forms a constellation I can see far more clearly than I can the Big Dipper. And it is true that we recently learned that the lead content in the mini-brownfield that is our backyard means there will be no vegetable garden this summer. Still, nature lets me know it is here every second, relentlessly bursting through the seams in the sidewalk, storing nuts in the walls of my attic, leaving little blessings on my windshield.

I hope I'll live long enough to chart an atlas of my backyard. I'll chart a gazetteer of the tender undulations of the landscape from inch to inch, the moist rivulets that are the earthworm's world map. I'll write a romance novel depicting the passion of the maple for the wind and a dissertation on the wanderlust of the creeping charley.

I was raised to know that I am responsible for tending my yard, not just for myself and the neighborhood, but for the bugs and beasts with whom I share it. My backyard is a tiny land trust, and I pronounce myself the honorary conservation officer for this little lot. As long as I'm here, the flock is safe, the mice will not be evicted from the garage, and the dandelions will never taste poison. I may even let the little lawn go to the prairie, though it would surely incite the ire of my neighbors—seedlings of "weeds" flitting about as if they were wild. As if this were wilderness.

Margaret Miles's family has lived in the Twin Cities for many generations. Margaret grew up in St. Paul and currently lives in Minneapolis's Whittier neighborhood, where she is a freelance writer. While she revels in planting her tent in prairie grasses, canoeing the Boundary Waters, and hiking Sugarloaf Bluff, she claims to be irrevocably a child of the urban wilderness.

My Lost Paradise

Mai Nguyen Haselman
2nd Place

I grew up in a beautiful home not far from Saigon. It wasn't a castle, or even a huge house, yet to me that house my dad designed and helped build was my little paradise. It was surrounded by tall walls with tiny sparkling stones to protect us from the outside world. My brothers and sister couldn't wait to get home after school every day so we could play with each other. We invented fairy-tale stories, and there were always enough of us to have a queen, a king, a prince, a princess, and even a little soldier. My father believed that a home is not a home until you bring nature in as much as possible, and with that in mind he transformed a small area around the walls into a garden with lush green trees and gorgeous blooming tropical flowers of a variety of colors. We played all day long under the shade trees, climbed up and played hide and seek under the mangos, rolled around on the soft green grass, which we had driven for hours out of Saigon to find and bring back. We ran under the hottest sun and—during the monsoon season—danced in the longest cold rains in Asia. At night we would sit under the bright full moon and bathe ourselves in the beautiful aroma of lovely white camellias. Life was as innocent as a baby's first smile. War was never a real word in our vocabulary.

Within a few years after the fall of Saigon, somehow we got settled in Minnesota. To us, June was too cool without a sweater and January was unbearable. I cried myself to sleep for the first several months and dreamed of flying back to our homeland to dance again in our little paradise. Slowly, we learned to adapt to our new life. We were like tiny seeds that someone brought back from a trip overseas and buried deep down in the rich new soil. My father showed us how to reach high and open ourselves to let the sun shine in; we would not have survived if he hadn't.

He worked days and nights to give us another home, a small piece of land in Minnetonka. Time flew by, and before we knew it, my father had slowly transformed the area surrounding our new house into a beautiful garden. In the summer, we would gather in the backyard, our own children sitting on the lush green grass or running around to touch and smell the lovely flowers. We watched the blue sky framed by the deep walls of tall evergreen he'd planted years ago, and ate the sweet plumbs picked fresh right off the tree. The smell of grape leaves on the grill blended with sweet corn to fill the air with love. Somehow, watching our children rolling around in the grass, running up and down the hill under an old maple tree, took me back to the little queen, king, prince, and princess playing in that forgotten paradise. Memories came and went like the gentle breezes. My father sat quietly, watching us under a shade tree with a look of great happiness on his face.

He passed away a few months ago, and we had to wait until a mountain of white snow thawed before we could go back and dream in his lovely garden. We saw rainbows appear in the coldest time in December just following his funeral. The intense colors of those rainbows were somehow like the flowers surrounding his home.

Whenever I miss him now, I do not have to travel over the ocean, back to our beautiful childhood, into our little paradise in Vietnam. My mind has only to go back to those summer days in Minnetonka, where we sat quietly under that old shady maple tree and watched the blue sky. He and I sat together like that for many days of the last summer of his life, both of us taking our surroundings into our hearts as much as possible, knowing that yet again our small world would soon never be the same.

What my father gave us was not some expensive gift that you can put in a box and gift wrap; rather, he gave us a life's dream with years of hard work and passion to re-create what we had lost long ago. And there it remains, our little paradise, safe forever in my heart. And this time, nobody can ever take it away from me.

Born in South Saigon, Vietnam, Mai Nguyen Haselman immigrated to the United States with her family in 1980. She wrote "My Lost Paradise" in memory of her father, her greatest hero, who recently passed away from lymphoma cancer. She is a proud mother of two and currently lives in Lino Lakes, Minnesota.

The Nature Lady

Barbara Lewis
3rd Place

I moved to a suburb of Minneapolis with the birth of my first child in '84. It was our first home, and we were so excited to have our own place. I remember the new home development on an old farmer's potato field north of the city. The plan included many drainage ponds and open areas between the houses, a rather new idea at the time. The lot we chose was on one of those little ponds, with brown dirt leading to its edge. It didn't look like much at the time, but we were city kids, and to us it was the Taj Mahal.

Once all the lots were built and our pond was surrounded by fresh green sod and a few promising young saplings, the view became one of pristine suburban order. The new neighbors gathered at backyard picnics and congratulated each other on the little landscape designs that so masterfully placed tiny trees and gardens in perfect relation to the pond.

Then about three years on, the first neighbor moved away, and in moved the Nature Lady. She was older than the rest of us, and she brought with her full-size indigenous trees and plants, huge boulders, and fountains! It was too much: her yard looked to us like a wild forest. Worse was the way she took over the pond; nature is bold, but she was bolder. She told the neighborhood children to stock the pond with toads and frogs and any other "nasty" little animals they could find. She guarded the natural willows and other weeds that grew precociously at the water's edge as though they were precious babies. We were all convinced by then that she was strange, but what took the cake was the day she chased away city mowers whose job it was to keep our pristine little pond pristine!

It was when all the cattails really started to grow that the neighbors finally revolted. We blamed her for turning our pretty little pond into a wild unruly unattractive reed bed. From shore to shore, cattails, cattails, and more cattails! I pacified my anger by imagining them blowing gently with the wind, much like the water did on the days I could even see it.

Three years went by, and as the cattails started thinning, I grew interested in the activity of all the little animals, which were delighting the children now, animals I had never really seen before—muskrats, rabbits, and squirrels. A devoted birdwatcher, I started feeding the many birds that had gathered in our yard, and counted more than thirty different species that stopped at our pond each year, my favorites being the great blue heron, the egret, and the red-winged blackbird with its trilling song.

The Nature Lady moved away, and it took me several more years before I really understood the incredible wealth of gifts she had given us. My little suburban home was rich with natural treasures I had been too shallow to appreciate in my youth. Thank you, Nature Lady: I have learned.

Barbara Lewis is an artist, a mother of teenagers, a busy arts volunteer, and an avid nature lover. She has planted a few trees and rocks of her own, and says she can be found in her wild unruly gardens most summer days.

Southern Region

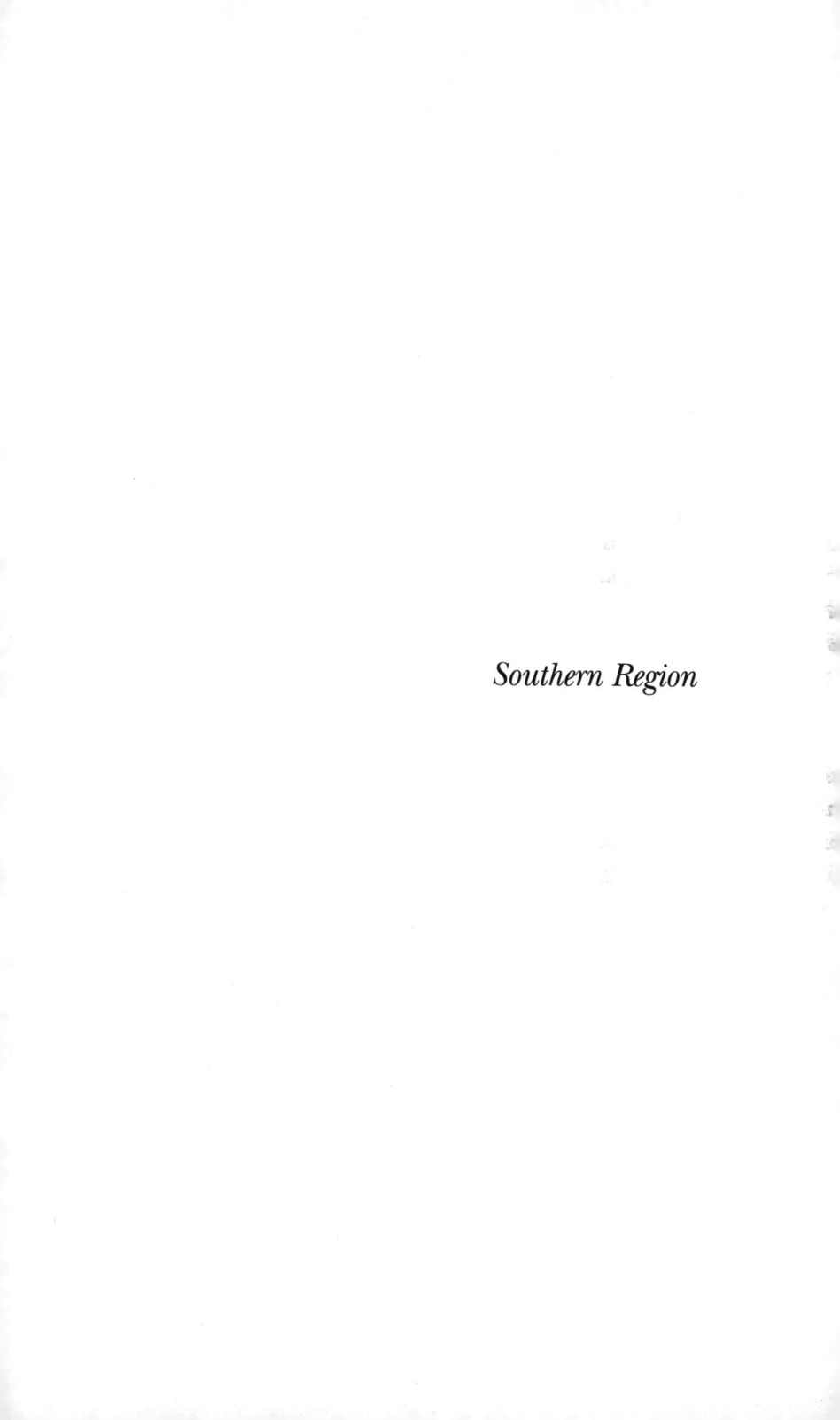

The Teachers

Florence Dacey

She remembers the wind in the tall grass beside the lake, where waves and yellow water lilies taught freedom and impermanence. Of course, there was her mother to name the everyday beauty: peony, iris, lilac. And her father in overalls leading her into a barn where a cat light-footed it among the soft placid cows. Golden straw, manure, meadowlark, cornstalk, snake. How could one not learn to love that intimacy whose worst wounding was a soon forgotten sting?

Soon the painters and writers arrived in her life, to illuminate the shining or shadowed corners of the starry sky, an illusive whale she still hasn't spied, a mystic haystack or ravishing garden transformed by light. There were layers of presences inside the colors and words. They informed her, so she could bring the wide lens of imagination to the natural world.

As much as the various landscapes, people showed her how to speak and act for the earth's sake. She witnessed a fourth-grader in an urban school write a poem in defense of wolves he had never seen; heard an old farmer in a nursing home tell his story of living more simply on the land; and always the women, who hold the memory of generations, taught her how we cannot escape our dependence on the earth, where we must learn to live in the body of flesh and spirit as if it were water, the dark iris, the open field.

Passion alone is not enough, she saw, though without it, we falter. A community of people with persistence, sophisticated political sense, and practical determination must struggle and celebrate together. She learned close-up how the everyday people of southwest Minnesota could speak truth to the experts, even as she listened through her computer to the voices of Greenpeace activists bobbing on some distant ocean.

And still the goldfinch and flicker, the backyard abundance, and the faraway seas go on teaching what it means to sing at dawn, flare like a firefly at night, disappear in fog. A multitude of oaks and ecologists, botanists and blizzards, grandmothers and guardians keep pointing the way. The reasons to nurture and protect this earth, sung daily by the wren, are now as familiar as her own skin. When she helps defend flowers, birds, trees, and rivers, it seems she defends herself. What would her life be, without the deep lake of freedom, the vast prairie of discovery, without the old tree daily revealing how to live and die?

Florence Dacey is a poet, creative writing teacher, and community arts and intergenerational programming consultant. She has lived in Cottonwood in southwest Minnesota for thirty-one years. Her environmental work has included numerous artist-in-residence projects about nature, especially rivers.

Prairie Marsh Farm

Jason M. Frank
Age 16

There is a farm owned by Goodman and Marge Larson of Hopkins in rural Lac qui Parle County, a few miles southwest of Madison, Minnesota. It is a very special farm that grows wildlife, wetlands, and historic prairie heritage.

The landscape is graced with gently rolling hills, immense fields of tallgrass prairie, pristine ponds and marshes, and bird-filled groves of spruce, box elder, walnut, and crabapple trees. The old red farmhouse is warm and inviting. And the barn, which was once the home of horses and cattle, now serves as the nesting site for barn swallows, who in spring and summer cheerily flitter above the farmyard, catching insects on the wing. Meadowlarks, perching on fence posts, sing their charming flutelike song, a welcomed melody drifting over the prairie on summer mornings. The majestic red-tailed hawk soars overhead; a flock of white pelicans lands on the marsh. And when the sun goes down, a chorus of crickets and frogs adds music to the quiet night.

In autumn, when the air becomes brisk and the mornings leave frost on big bluestem, ducks and geese from the far north land on the area wetlands. While hunting pheasants and waterfowl last October, my dad and I estimated ten thousand ducks circling over the eighty-acre slough as the sun was rising. This slough, a few miles away from Prairie Marsh Farm, is also a haven for pheasants. The scenic hills of South Dakota rise over the western horizon, and red-winged blackbirds gather in the reeds and sing to greet the morning. During the evening you may hear the deep, foreshadowing hoot of the great horned owl.

When the snows arrive, normally in mid- to late-November, the landscape is completely transformed. Memories of an old-fashioned country Christmas enter one's mind. One of the most beautiful sights in nature is fluffy snow on evergreen boughs and prairie grass.

Perhaps just as beautiful are the sounds of winter songbirds that visit the bird feeders: chickadees, juncos, sparrows, woodpeckers, and nuthatches. The abundance of white-tailed deer on Prairie Marsh Farm is even more evident in winter, when one can see their tracks in the snow, leading from one grove to the next.

Prairie Marsh Farm, an ecological haven, a very special place indeed.

Jason Frank is sixteen years old and lives on a hobby farm in rural Isanti county. Jason likes to hunt, fish, camp, read, write, birdwatch, and just be outdoors. He entered this essay contest because he has always been interested in Minnesota's natural history.

Marsh Song

Robert Hartkopf
1st Place

The first attempt to drain the marsh was made with a horse-drawn dredge in 1910. It failed. The marsh, although diminished, survived for the next fifty years. That's when I entered the picture.

I was born during the Depression in an old farmhouse near the banks of the eight hundred-acre marsh. My earliest memories are of ducks and geese cascading over the farmyard before spiraling into the marsh. At dusk, thousands of waterfowl flew from the Minnesota River bottoms to spend nights on its sheltered waters. Musical sounds of trumpeting, whirring, and whistling wafted through the night air to enrich our lives.

Whether family members were outdoors or indoors, the marsh beckoned. One of the kitchen windows faced the marsh, which made it the most looked-out-of window in the weathered gray house. Exclamations like, "Come see!" "Look!" and "Hurry!" abounded because of the living panorama that window offered. But it was not to last.

Drainage fever reached another peak in the late fifties, and huge earthmoving machines were ready and waiting. Several farmers petitioned to repair the 1910 ditch. With little regard for ditching laws, engineers and contractors widened and deepened the original ditch and all surface water drained out of the marsh into the Minnesota River.

Years later, in 1991, nature returned water to the empty marsh basin with a vengeance. I spent Halloween of that year in the same hundred-year-old farmhouse I had lived in as a boy. On that sleepless Halloween night, I peered through the kitchen window and reminisced for hours as torrential rain turned to wet, blinding snow. I knew the marsh basin would temporarily flood. At the stormy dawn, I trudged through knee-deep snow in high anticipation. Reaching the bank brought total disbelief. Instead of water lapping at the shore, I saw what appeared to be eight hundred acres of black plowed fields. My senses screamed, *"This can't be!"*

Suddenly the entire basin exploded into a black cloud. Tens of thousands of migrating Canada geese had descended during the raging blizzard and blanketed the water. Their thundering wings and clamoring calls were the same wild, wondrous music heard years before. A dream soared with the geese. If restored, the marsh would sing again. And maybe, just maybe, it will.

Robert Hartkopf describes himself as an ecologist, filmmaker, and organic gardener. He spent his boyhood on a farm adjacent to a marsh. When the marsh was drained, he filmed "Cry of the Marsh" to document the destruction and has been working with environmental groups ever since to preserve and restore marshlands.

The Oak Grove

Eve Webster
2nd Place

A band of lakes, broadcast like blue seed, reaches across the prairie of west-central Minnesota. Below it lies the Alexandria Moraine. It is a young, hard landscape scraped and carved by ice that retreated just ten thousand years ago. The glacial debris that remains, some of the deepest in the state, ranges ten to twenty miles across. From Detroit Lakes the moraine runs south to Willmar, then curves east. Eventually, the swish of western wheat grass and rustle of burr oak gives voice to this land.

My parents bought a farm on the southern edge of the Alexandria Moraine during the Great Depression. In my childhood there was little talk of kame or kettle, no mention of moraine. What mattered, voices implied, was the surface, the fields and prairie pastures.

Forty acres of white and burr oaks stood on drumlin and hollow between us and our northern neighbors. The woods stoked our furnace and sheltered our farmyard from northwest winds. My father's voice capitalized *Oak Grove,* as if it were the name of a neighbor. Whenever he found reason to walk the woods, I tagged along. There was little need for conversation.

In a great white oak, my father and I found bees whose honey tasted of buckwheat. We sampled chokecherries and bittersweet plums while avoiding the nettle and cockleburs. On my own I gathered acorns, caught painted turtles, and cheered on our dogs when they chased raccoons into shallow woodland ponds. In spring and fall, I observed courtships of all kinds.

One moonlit winter night my father pointed to snow swept by the splayed feathers of a widespread wing. We followed tracks that feinted left, then right. Again, a wing had struck the snow. The tracks widened, a sign of fear. Another wing sweep. Then suddenly, a struggle and darkened snow. We talked that night about the victim, about the victor's hunger, about survival. In words unspoken, my father said, "This is life, both ending and beginning."

My father has been gone awhile now. The oak grove, bulldozed by the next owner, has been reduced to yet another soybean field. My head says, Memory is enough. But when my heart says it's not, I return to the parks that preserve the ancient-newborn landscape of the Alexandria Moraine. There, for me, time and space, sound and shape, are once again a seamless whole.

Eve Webster is a retired Northfield attorney who enjoys writing, reading, backpacking, and sailing. She and her husband travel frequently and recently biked down the Danube from Passau to Vienna. Eve serves on several philanthropic boards and last year helped create Wings, a women's endowment fund, in Northfield. The Websters have two children and are expecting their first grandchild.

The Sight of a Lifetime

Rod Broding
3rd Place

Hunched over like the outdoor warrior he was, my dad slowly crept ahead of me toward our destination. His hand gestured me to come forward, but a finger laid upon his lips cautioned me not to make any noise. Dad was about to show me a special fishing spot.

Adjacent to what used to be the Showboat Ballroom, a small pond fed its spring runoff into Lake Benton through a watery ribbon not more than three feet wide and a foot deep. It was Dad's favorite spot from which to spear those early spring suckers. What made it so enticing for the spear-fisherman was a grassy bank about three feet high on one side of that narrow creek, which enabled the adversary to sneak up on their prey and carefully peek over the bank's edge to see how many suckers were wallowing their way into the pond to spawn.

On an early spring morning, this boy of twelve, with great anticipation, crawled toward that coveted precipice until my eyes could peer over the edge of that bank. I was ready, spear in hand. But I was not ready for what greeted me.

"Oh, my gosh!" Dad exclaimed. Like a huge battleship, a northern pike, no less than twenty pounds, cruised nearly motionless through the channel right beneath our eyes! I could almost reach out and touch it—a fish so large that the morning sun glistened off its wet back protruding from the water.

In spellbound silence, father and son watched Battleship Northern slowly glide toward her destination, unhindered and unperturbed. In a moment of reverence I set my spear aside and pondered the significance of this event. I felt Dad's warm hand on my back as if to keep me in a prone position. "The sight of a lifetime!" Dad whispered. Indeed, it was!

Both Dad and the showboat are gone now; the land lays idle waiting for some developer, I suppose. But for me, this place is unique, and I want to save it. Why shouldn't it become the newest Lincoln County Park, that all might enjoy the sandy beach and rocky outcropping that constitute its shoreline? Then, maybe another youngster might someday peer over that bank's edge and experience the "sight of a lifetime."

Rod Broding's childhood was spent mostly outdoors in the communities of Lake Benton and Pipestone. Married to Marilyn Keehr and the father of three adult children, Rod enjoys fishing with his kids and six grandchildren. Rod, who now lives in Coon Rapids, is the author of Tacklebox of Hope, *a book of devotions for the Christian fisherman. His dream is to retire "on the lake" near Battle Lake.*

*You are invited to become one of
1000 Friends of Minnesota*

Why Minnesota Needs 1000 Friends:

Minnesota is one of the fastest growing states in America. It is important that our growth be sensible and careful. We must balance our state's rapid growth with a concern for the environment and plan growth to fit within the traditional quality of life Minnesotans enjoy.

Why 1000 Friends of Minnesota Needs You:

We are a membership organization that depends on the contributions of people like you. We need your support if we are to continue our important work. Minnesota is beautiful, with abundant and diverse resources: from prairies to forests, to blufflands, to lakes and rivers. Our cities rank among the most beautiful and livable in the nation. We must protect this quality of life. We are committed to this effort. Please call us or see our website for membership information.

1000 Friends of Minnesota
370 Selby Avenue, Suite 300
St. Paul, MN 55102
651-312-1000
www.1000fom.org